<u>A Trip To The Country</u>

Nature in Rhyme

By: **Elizabeth Eugenia I. Kapp**

Illustrations by: **Kirsten Julia Kapp**

Editing by: **Matthew Chandler Kapp**

AuthorHouse™
1663 Liberty Drive
Bloomington, IN 47403
www.authorhouse.com
Phone: 1 (800) 839-8640

Published by AuthorHouse 10/06/2016

ISBN: 978-1-5246-3815-3 (sc)
ISBN: 978-1-5246-3817-7 (hc)
ISBN: 978-1-5246-3816-0 (e)

Library of Congress Control Number: 2016914668

Print information available on the last page.

Any people depicted in stock imagery provided by Thinkstock are models,
and such images are being used for illustrative purposes only.
Certain stock imagery © Thinkstock.

This book is printed on acid-free paper.

Because of the dynamic nature of the Internet, any web addresses or links contained in this book may have changed
since publication and may no longer be valid. The views expressed in this work are solely those of the author and do not
necessarily reflect the views of the publisher, and the publisher hereby disclaims any responsibility for them.

authorHOUSE®

For: Cayden Kapp Paulson to learn about nature and appreciate poetry.

Dedication

To: Laura Goodyear, who first introduced me to poetry

and

*My father, Carl Gailord Kapp, for urging me to write, and
My mother, Julia Constance Kapp, for her inspiration.*

Once there was a little girl named Kirsten. She was four years old and she had an older brother named Matty, who was seven. They loved to play in their backyard, which had swings, a sandbox and a lovely flower garden with purple lilac bushes growing along a fence. There was also a very tall weeping willow tree that they loved to sit under.

Birds of all kinds sang their different songs from the nearby oak and maple trees.

Cute bunny rabbits hopped about the lawn and many pretty butterflies floated through the air.

On this particular day the children played while their parents packed the car for a trip to the country to see their sick grandmother. Kirsten was wearing a pretty yellow organdy pinafore dress with wing-like shoulders. She looked at her dress, then looked at the fluttery yellow butterflies and thought perhaps she was supposed to be a butterfly too. She flapped her arms, jumped up, and twirled around trying desperately to stay in the air, but each time she came down with a thud and so decided she wasn't meant to be a butterfly after all. She asked Matty, "What makes them fly and why can't I?" Matty said that Mother told him:

Gravity

A force called <u>gravity</u> keeps us on the ground
Otherwise we'd all be flying around
And apples would fall up instead of down
If it weren't for gravity we wouldn't weigh a pound
(Some ladies would really like that I've found)
And you're not made like a butterfly
With fast fluttering wings to move you up high

Kirsten was disappointed but turned her attention to the flowers in the garden, which she loved. She had asked her mother all about them.

Flowers

Mother can you tell me
Why are the flowers here?
Oh, yes they are so pretty
Just like you my dear

They are gifts from heaven
Pollinated by birds and bees
I think that they were sent
Just for us to please

In this garden are snaps and roses
Along with phlox and sweet peas
See the daffodils and iris
And tulips, lilies, and peonies

What makes them grow up mother?
Tall and pretty and strong?
Sunshine, rain and fertilizer
Help to bring them along

And what happens to them in winter?
Do they die and disappear?
No, many stay in the ground down under
Then they bloom again next year.

Kirsten noticed that the grass was all wet but that it hadn't rained. Matty explained that the grass was covered with dew because it was still early morning.

He said, as he was digging up the earth:

Dew

At night when you are sleeping
And all the stars are keeping
Safe watch down over you
The grass grows heavy, full of dew
The water in the air forms droplets
Which <u>condense</u> to form a toplet
Like a cover on the ground
Later on it is not found
For when the sun warms up the air
Dewdrops <u>evaporate</u> and disappear.

Matty kept on digging in the ground because he was told: "If you dig straight down, you can find China."

A gentle breeze made the long willows sway easily on the tree above them. Matty said: "The breeze comes from":

Wind

Air always moves around the world
Some is warm and some is cold
Warm air rises up from the <u>equator</u>
Cold flows below from the region <u>polar</u>
The moving air that we call wind
Has different <u>velocities</u> that on temperature depend
And that's just about all I know
About the wind and breezes that blow.

"Mother's calling," said Matty. We have to go now. Kirsten said "O.K.," although she really wanted so much to keep playing and not sit in the car for hours. She was happy though, for Matty had just found "China"—pieces of a cup and saucer in the pretty Willowware pattern.

Off they all went. On and off the parkway, through the mountains and fresh smelling air, past some streams and on to Grandma's. She was in a nursing home. They were going to stay at Aunt Betsy's nearby cottage on Fishing Creek.

On the way to the cottage it began to rain and there was thunder and lightning in the sky. "What makes it rain?" asked Matt. Daddy answered:

Rain

Hot air rises up above
Meets with cool and then drops down
Making puddles that you love
As the rain falls to the ground

"What makes those loud noises?" said Kirsten, looking very frightened. "Don't worry," said Aunt Betsy, "It won't hurt us. Thunder is just"-----

Thunder

Lightning heats the air in its path
Which expands so very fast
It causes an enormous blast
That's why we call it thunder
Thunder and lightning happen together
Though we first see one, then hear the other.

"What makes lightning ?" asked Matty. Mother replied:

Lightning

When you look up in the sky
And see great big clouds way high
Know you may soon have home to run
For surely rain's about to come
And from those large <u>*cumulonimbus*</u> *clouds*
Lightning may flash up and down
From the air and water which whirl and crash
Causing electrical charges to build then flash
Don't be afraid, lightning's safe to see
But it's not wise to sit under a tree

After they arrived at Aunt Betsy's cozy cottage, they lit a fire in the fireplace and had some hot chocolate to take off the chill. They looked out the window to watch the raindrops falling one by one on the creek just below, each drop leaving circles surrounding it in the water. "Why are the circles there?" asked Kirsten.
Daddy answered:

Centrifugal

*There's a force of which I've heard others speak
When raindrops fall into the creek
Circles form around every drop
The circles keep going and do not stop
Centrifugal causes the circles to go round
And always in a pattern outward bound.*

Soon it was time for Aunt Betsy's best meatloaf and Waldorf salad supper. Afterward they sang some songs like "On Moonlight Bay" and "Now Is the Hour," while Aunt Betsy played the piano. Then they went up to bed on the screened-in sleeping porch. There they could see bright stars overhead and listen to the sound of a nearby waterfall and the hoot of an owl. Matty asked, "Why can we see stars and fireflies at night?" Mother said:

Light

From the porch we can see stars at night
Some of them are very bright
Each gives off its own light to guide us
Just like fireflies, both are called <u>luminous</u>
Light does travel so very fast
Its future is nearly the same as its past
Light travels in a direct line down
If it travels the equator around
In one second it circles seven and one-half times
Now it's time for sleep, we've finished today's rhymes.

In the morning, Mother and Daddy went to see Grandma. Matty and Kirsten stayed at the cottage and learned to skip stones across the creek, then helped Aunt Betsy water the flowers in her window boxes. Kirsten asked Aunt Betsy this time, "What makes flowers?" Aunt Betsy said:

Flowers Turn Their Faces

The flowers turn their faces
Right up into the sun
The birds and bees then take their places
Kissing each and every one
And so they spread the <u>pollen</u>
After they've taken a drink
Well that's what someone told me
And that's just what I think
That's why we have new flowers
And not just the old
Just like new little babies
For mothers' arms to hold.

Later Matty and Kirsten went digging for worms to use for bait to catch fish. Afterward, they went in the rowboat to one of the small islands on the creek where they enjoyed a nice swim, then built a fire on the pebbly shore and had delicious hot dogs and baked beans for lunch.

Matty had thought they should go to the island when it was low tide so they wouldn't be washed away in the high water. Aunt Betsy explained that he needn't worry because there were very low tides at the creek, since it was fresh water and not salt water like in the ocean. Of course Matty wanted to know why there were different tides and Aunt Betsy explained:

Tides

The moon has <u>gravity</u> just like the earth
It pulls on the water for all it's worth
And that's why the water rises up high
When the earth, moon and sun are lined up in the sky
Very high tide comes when the moon is just new
Or else when the full moon is in view

After lunch Matty was so happy to catch a catfish and some perches, which they would fry in a pan and have for dinner later, when Mother and Daddy returned from seeing Grandma.

The next morning they picked some flowers for Grandma and then they all went to see her. She was very weak, but she managed to smile sweetly at the children as each one gave her greetings and the flowers they brought.

After a little while she fell asleep and they all decided to say goodbye for the day, when the nurse came in to take her pulse. There simply wasn't any. Everything was very quiet. "She's passed on," said the nurse.

Mother and Daddy were very sad. Aunt Betsy said that Grandma had died and gone to heaven and they wouldn't see her again—at least not for a very long time. Mother explained what heaven was, and all about the angels that would take her there.

It rained during the sad car journey back to Aunt Betsy's from the nursing home, but after a while it rained less and the sun came out. Kirsten looked up through the car window and saw the most beautiful arch of many different colors stretching across the sky from horizon to horizon.

"What is that?" asked Kirsten. Mother explained that the arch was called a rainbow, saying:

Rainbow

You can see a rainbow
If your back is to the sun
Which shines upon the raindrops
Showing seven colors in a <u>spectrum</u>
Scientifically that's the story
And there's a heavenly tale too
That God sent a sign to Noah
After the flood he led him through
Some say it is a curtain
Lovely colored and sheer
Separating us from animal heaven
Where bunnies hop higher than here
And I've also heard it said
That many have often told
At the rainbow's very end
Is a great big pot of gold!

Matty grinned up at the rainbow and in a loud voice yelled: "Yay, it's a sign that Grandma made it into heaven." And all the sad faces, including Kirsten, smiled big smiles and were very happy knowing Grandma was with God.

GLOSSARY

Centrifugal Force   The force experienced in a body moving along a curved path and appearing to propel the body outward.

Condense   Turn from gas or vapor into liquid or solid state.

Cumulonimbus   Billowing storm clouds that stretch high up into the sky.

Evaporate   To change from a liquid or solid state into vapor.

Equator   Imaginary circle around earth equidistant from the poles.

Gravity   Force of attraction of one body for another, such as objects pulled toward the center of the earth.

Luminous   Bright; glowing; radiating or reflecting light; shining.

Polar   Of or pertaining to the North or South Pole. Regions within The Arctic and Antarctic circles.

Pollen   Yellow fertilizing dust of a flower.

Pollination   To convey pollen to a flower.

Spectrum   The range of different colors produced when light passes through a glass prism or drop of water.

Velocities   Rapidity of motion, action, or operation. Swiftness; speed.

The real Kirsten and Matty

Acknowledgements

A thousand thanks to my illustrator and niece, Kirsten Kapp, for her diligence, skill, and ability to organize her many other responsibilities, in order to make this book come alive. Another thousand to my editor and nephew, Matthew Kapp, for applying his photography and editorial skills, along with excellent advice for this book project.

Without the support of John Tuttle, this book would not have been possible, and it is so much appreciated; as is also the support of Alex Petrovsky.

Many thanks also to the late Evelyn Miller, Linda and Bruce Kapp, Richard Foody and Karen Stansberry, (Publishing Consultant for Authorhouse); for their patience in reading and critiquing my manuscript.

Elizabeth has written numerous poems, some of which have been published in *World of Poetry Anthology* and other books, as well as in a European newspaper along with television coverage.

A human resources management professional, Elizabeth has undergraduate and graduate degrees in psychology, sociology, and human resources management. She is a native of Elizabeth, New Jersey, and now resides in New York City.

Printed in the United States
By Bookmasters